ERYL the PERIL

MEREDITH COSTAIN

Illustrated by Ian Forss

For Sam and Susannah

Written by Meredith Costain
Illustrated by Ian Forss

Published by Mimosa Publications Pty Ltd
PO Box 779, Hawthorn 3122, Australia
© 1995 Mimosa Publications Pty Ltd
All rights reserved

Literacy 2000 is a Trademark registered in the
United States Patent and Trademark Office.

Distributed in the United States of America by

Rigby
A Division of Reed Elsevier Inc.
500 Coventry Lane
Crystal Lake, IL 60014
800-822-8661

Distributed in Canada by
PRENTICE HALL GINN
1870 Birchmount Road
Scarborough
Ontario M1P 2J7

99 98
10 9 8 7 6 5 4 3

Printed in Hong Kong through Bookbuilders Ltd

ISBN 0 7327 1567 9

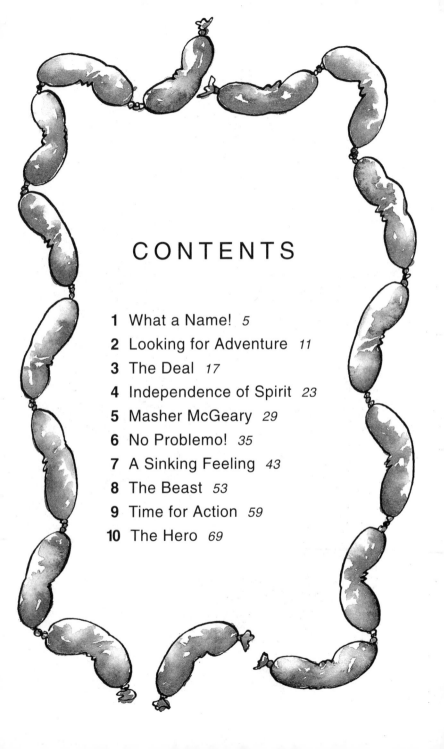

CONTENTS

1
What a Name!

Errol Finn hated his name. Errol. It sounded stupid. The kids at school all called him Errol the Peril. It wasn't fair. Why couldn't his parents have chosen an ordinary name? Like Tom, or Pete, or even Jeremy. *Anything* but Errol.

Errol was the type of kid who was always getting into trouble. Not because he'd misbehaved, though. With Errol it wasn't that kind of trouble. It was more because he had a good imagination. He'd pretend to be someone really exciting, like a prize-winning author or a brilliant scientist, when he was meant to be doing his schoolwork. So instead of quietly doing a multiplication problem like the other students, he'd be dreaming up an amazing new scientific formula that would miraculously cure every known disease; or he'd be heading a brave expedition into territory considered so dangerous that no one had yet ventured there; or he'd be writing an acceptance speech for the Nobel Prize.

When Errol walked across the school playground, he was so busy plotting this plan, or hatching that scheme, that he often bumped right into other kids, or even into teachers. "Watch out," cried the kids, as they tried to avoid collisions, "here comes Errol the Peril!"

It was even worse when he played sports. Take last Wednesday, when he'd finally been picked to play baseball. Baseball was really popular at Errol's school. The kids rushed out every lunchtime with bats and balls. They would shout and cheer as balls were sent flying over the fence. The winners would throw their caps high into the air at the end of a game and laugh and slap each other on the back. (The losers usually threw their caps down on the ground in disgust!)

Errol usually just watched the other kids play. He was considered too much of a klutz to be picked for a team. But last Wednesday, he *had* been picked – by Kate James. Besides being the best baseball player, Kate James was also the toughest kid in school. So being picked to play on her side was a real honor.

But everything had gone wrong. When Rocky Zotz hit a ball high in his direction,

Errol didn't even see it coming. He was too busy dreaming about standing up on the dais at the Olympic Games, collecting a gold medal for baseball. He dropped the catch. His team lost by one run. And Errol handed his glove in sadly and went back to sitting on the bench.

The kids on his team had thrown their caps on the ground grudgingly at the end of the game. Errol could have stamped

his cap right into the ground. "Errol the Peril," the kids chanted, as they trooped back into school when the bell rang.

Errol wasn't really sure what "peril" meant, but he had a feeling it probably wasn't a very nice thing to call someone, even if it did happen to rhyme with Errol. So he looked up "peril" in the dictionary. "Danger" it said. "Jeopardy." "Risk." And to do something "at your peril" meant to live dangerously. Hmm, maybe Errol the Peril wasn't such a bad name after all!

Then one day his grandma told him that he'd been named after a great movie star, Errol Flynn, and not only was this Errol guy a great star, he was the type of actor who always had great adventures. Swashbuckling pirate adventures on the high seas. Spectacular sword fights against deadly enemies, two at a time. Perilous adventures in fighter planes in skies blackened with storm clouds and lit up only by giant flashes of lightning.

So, Errol thought, he really did have a name that went along with danger and excitement. Yes, and with a name

like his, it was about time he had a few adventures of his own. If Flynn could do it, why not Finn? Just thinking about it made him quiver with excitement. He'd start right now!

2
Looking for Adventure

"Mo-o-om?"

Mrs. Finn was peeling vegetables at the sink. She'd come home late from work and had a headache. Errol was always asking questions and she had a fair idea he was about to ask another.

"Ask your father," she said, waving him away with a carrot.

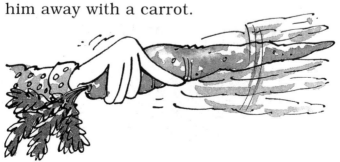

Mr. Finn was slicing a piece of meat into cubes. He was concentrating very hard to make sure he didn't cut his finger with the sharp knife. (He was already nursing two flesh wounds from last night's dinner.) "Da-a-ad?" said Errol.

"Ask your grandma," Errol's father said, the knife coming dangerously close to his little finger.

Grandma was in the middle of a 5000-piece jigsaw puzzle of the Grand Canyon. She always had plenty of time for Errol, even when he asked very complicated questions that you couldn't answer unless you looked in an encyclopedia.

Errol sat down next to her on the couch. He pushed one tiny brown piece of jigsaw up against another tiny brown piece.

"Not there, dear," said Grandma, but she didn't sound annoyed. Not like his

dad had when Errol accidentally drowned his pet Mexican walking fish in the golf-ball cleaner. Now *that* was annoyed.

"Oh," said Errol, "sorry." The brown pieces all looked the same to him. And just look at all those tiny blue pieces of sky, all blurring into one before his eyes. He couldn't see how she'd ever finish it.

He sat up very straight, and stroked his skin just below his nose, where his mustache would be if he were the great Errol Flynn.

"Grandma," he said boldly, "I need an adventure."

"That's nice, dear," said Grandma, choosing another brown piece. "What kind of adventure did you have in mind?"

Errol hadn't thought about that part yet. He closed his eyes and played some adventures on the screen in his mind. An archeologist in the Amazon Basin, being chased by natives? A star trooper, risking his life to save the planet from invading, ten-headed aliens with slimy, wandering tentacles? A . . .

"When I was a young girl," declared Grandma, clicking another piece of her puzzle into place, "I went camping."

"Camping?" said Errol.

"There's nothing quite like it," said Grandma firmly, "for adventure." She stood up and shuffled into the bathroom.

Errol bent down and picked
up some puzzle pieces that
had dropped on the floor.

Camping, of course! It was bound to
be dripping with adventure. Grandma
hadn't mentioned any movies where Errol
Flynn had gone camping, but that didn't
matter. He'd make his own fun.

There was an old tent in the back of
the hall closet. He and his sister Scarlett
(another movie name, Grandma said) had

used the tent to play Explorers when they were little. There were probably other things lying around – things you took with you on camping expeditions – that he could dig out as well.

Camping, huh? It sounded great.

He'd go tomorrow.

3
The Deal

Errol called his best friend, Sam. "You doing anything very interesting this weekend?" he asked casually.

"Dad wants me to weed the garden," replied Sam.

"Great," said Errol, relieved, "nothing important then."

"But he's paying me for doing the weeding," explained Sam, "*and* taking me to the ten-screen theater at the shopping center to see a horror movie."

This was stiff opposition. Errol knew how much Sam loved horror movies. He also knew Sam was saving up for a new computer game, so he wouldn't want to give up any chance of making some extra money.

"I'll tell you what," said Errol persuasively.

"Tell your dad I'll come around after school on Monday and help you with the weeding. We'll get twice as much done in half the time, and I won't even charge him for my work."

"Okay," conceded Sam, "that sounds fair. But what about the movie?"

"Believe me," crooned Errol, "what I've planned is ten times more exciting, thrilling, and enthralling than any old horror movie."

"Oh yes," said Sam. He knew all about Errol's schemes. Some of them were pretty crazy. "So what are you doing this time?"

Errol lowered his voice dramatically, "I'm going . . . camping."

"You're going where?" asked Sam.

"Camping!" said Errol brightly. His words tumbled out in a rush. "I've got the whole thing planned. We'll take our tent – it's really big and roomy – and make a campfire, and eat hot dogs and beans and chocolate and things . . ."

"Go on," said Sam. He just loved chocolate.

"And we'll be able to stay up as late as we want, and tell scary monster stories, and nobody big will be around to tell us what to do." Errol paused for a moment. This wasn't exactly true. His parents weren't likely to let him go off camping in any old place. No. They'd have to go to the place where he and his family had picnics every summer, at the back of Uncle Hector's farm. It was still pretty neat, though. "Well, not unless we want them to, anyway," he finished.

It all sounded good. Yes, very good. Sam was just about convinced. "But I really did want to see that movie . . ." he wheedled.

Errol hesitated exactly six seconds. "You can ride my new bike there," he said.

Sam smiled into the phone. Errol's bike was great. It was the latest, coolest mountain bike on the market. It had an aerodynamically designed seat, speed handlebars, and an amazing horn.

"We-ll . . ." said Sam. He didn't want to sound too eager. "What time do you want me to come over?"

Yay! thought Errol. He was actually going camping! "Eight o'clock tomorrow

morning," he said. "Make sure you bring your sleeping bag, and lots of food to cook on the campfire. And tons of . . ."

"Chocolate!" interrupted Sam. "No problemo. I'll be there, and don't forget – *I'm* riding your bike."

"No problemo," said Errol, hanging up the phone. He sighed. If he let Sam ride his bike, that meant he'd have to borrow his little sister's bike, "Li'l Blossom." It wasn't exactly the sort of thing Errol Flynn would ride into danger.

But who really cared? He was going camping, wasn't he? Sam and he were bound to have lots of adventures – more, probably, than you'd get in ten Errol Flynn movies put together!

4
Independence of Spirit

Mr. and Mrs. Finn were thrilled at the thought of the two boys going camping. It showed real "independence of spirit," they said.

Mr. Finn had poked around in the back of the refrigerator and the pantry for suitable food to eat on a camping trip. Mrs. Finn had taken a flashlight out to the garage and found her old canvas backpack, a ground cloth, and other useful things to take camping.

His parents were also full of all sorts of useful advice and helpful tips.

"Be sure to douse the fire whenever you leave it," said Mrs. Finn.

"Don't eat any berries or mushrooms you find in case they're poisonous," added Mr. Finn.

"Remember to tighten all the ropes on the tent in case there's a strong wind," said Mrs. Finn.

"Don't leave any garbage lying around for us to stumble over next time we're there," reminded Mr. Finn.

"And don't forget that if you have any problems at all, you're to let Uncle Hector know so that he can call us right away," said Mrs. Finn, gently stroking her son's spiky hair.

Errol sighed. "Yes, Mom," he said. He looked over at his grandma, who winked back at him.

"You boys are going to have a great time. I can feel it in my bones," she said. She reached deep into her cavernous purse and pulled out a brightly wrapped package. "I was saving this for Christmas, but you might as well have it now, dear," she said, handing it to Errol.

Errol unwrapped the colorful paper to find a genuine, all-purpose, heavy-duty explorer's watch. "Cool! Gee, thanks Grandma," he said, giving her a kiss. "This will be really good on the trip, for timing our adventures and things."

In fact, everything was looking pretty good, considering he'd only thought of the idea the night before. The sky was blue and cloudless. He had tons of great equipment. There was only one small, nagging problem: Li'l Blossom.

To get to the road that led out of town and to Uncle Hector's farm, he and Sam were going to have to ride past Masher McGeary's place. There was no way of avoiding it. If Masher saw him riding his little sister's pink and white bike, he'd never live it down.

Masher was the kind of kid who made himself feel big by making other people feel small. He was the one, for instance, who'd first added the "Peril" bit to Errol's name. Seeing Errol riding a girl's bike was just the sort of thing that Masher would make sure the whole school knew about. The very thought of it sent goose bumps down Errol's spine.

Still, Errol – like his namesake – was a man of his word. He had promised Sam his bike, and so he would have it. If only they didn't have to ride past Masher's place.

Sam arrived at eight o'clock on the dot, dressed in camouflage gear. He was carrying a super-featherlight sleeping bag and wearing hiking boots. He looked amazing.

"You look amazing!" breathed Errol, deeply envious.

"Thanks," said Sam modestly, as he collected Errol's super-cool mountain bike from the garage. "Looks like we're all set to go."

Errol heaved his mother's sturdy backpack up onto his back. It clinked a bit where Scarlett had tied a row of cooking implements to the side pockets. He put his father's lumpy sleeping bag into the basket and threw his leg over Li'l Blossom. "Affirmative," he said.

"Wait a minute, Err!" Mrs. Finn came running out of the house, carrying her aqua waterproof jacket. "Put this on, dear!" Errol gulped. An aqua jacket? On a pink and white bike? He'd rather die.

"You never know, it might rain. And it's always best to be prepared," clucked his mother, slipping off his backpack and settling the aqua folds into place around his shoulders.

Errol looked up at the sky. Still blue. One fluffy white cloud.

"Yes, Mom," he sighed. He gave the miniature kickstand a flick with his left foot. They were off!

5
Masher McGeary

"So, where exactly are we going?" asked Sam, coasting past Errol. He knew from experience that it was always wise to check these things out in advance. Once he'd gone off with Errol for a moonlight picnic and they'd ended up in the swamp at the back of the new shopping mall, flapping at mosquitoes as big as planes.

"Trust me," panted Errol. He had to pedal so fast to keep up that his legs were beginning to ache. The wheels on Li'l Blossom were a lot smaller than he was used to. "It's a special place. You're really going to like it."

"Hmm," said Sam. He'd packed some extra-strong bug repellent, just to be on the safe side.

The boys rounded the corner. They were heading for Masher McGeary's house. Errol took a long, deep breath and crossed his fingers over the handlebars. Maybe Mrs. McGeary had asked Masher to help with the housework or something and he'd be trapped inside, too busy to see them. Or maybe aliens had landed in the middle of the night, and decided to transport Masher back to their planet for scientific experimentation. Or maybe . . .

But there he was. Sitting on the fence out in front of his house, using a water pistol to terrorize the ants crawling along the path.

"Sam, quick," hissed Errol out of the corner of his mouth. "Keep your head down and ride straight by. Maybe he won't notice us."

But it was too late. Masher was already climbing off the fence. He strolled toward them, his smooth round face cracking with laughter.

"Well, it's my old pal, Peril," jeered Masher. "Going off for a tea party? Or maybe you're entering yourself in a best-dressed bike parade."

"Faster!" wheezed Errol to Sam.

"I *love* your jacket, Peril!" Masher snarled loudly. "The color looks *so* good on you."

"Faster! Faster!" cried Errol. He was now pedaling so fast he thought his legs would fly off the bike any minute and he'd be involved in a serious accident.

"See you Monday," shouted Masher, flexing his muscles. "I'll be waiting!"

Just my luck, thought Errol, his heart pounding. He'd have to spend all Monday hiding now. He could just imagine it: Big Mouth Masher McGeary telling every kid in the school about him riding along in an aqua jacket on a pink and white bike. He wished he had the courage to stand up to Masher. Errol Flynn certainly wouldn't let anyone laugh at him like that – not after all those swashbuckling pirate adventures and daring flying stunts.

He put his head down and began to pedal even faster. In only a few minutes

Masher was far behind them. He looked just like a little ant in the distance, and then became nothing more than a black speck on the fence. Errol cheered up at the thought of Masher growing smaller and smaller until he finally disappeared. Well, that might be too good to be true, but at least Masher was stuck at home. Sitting on a fence and shooting water at a few ants was pretty boring compared

to the kind of adventure he and Sam were about to have. He could hardly wait to get out into the countryside and set up the tent!

6
No Problemo!

"Errol," asked Sam, after they'd pedaled furiously for what seemed like hours, "how much farther is it? I'm starving. Can't we stop for a rest?"

Errol thought longingly of all the food that his father had so thoughtfully provided. He was hot and sweaty under the aqua jacket and his legs were aching. But there was no way he was going to let Sam know that.

He consulted his new heavy-duty all-purpose explorer's watch. Oops! According to the watch, it was only ten past eight! It must have stopped. Never mind. He'd learned at school that sailors could tell the time from the position of the sun in the sky. He squinted up, hoping to see something that would give him a clue.

Where had all those thick, dark clouds come from? What had happened to the one, small, fluffy white cloud and the clear, blue sky? And how long had they been riding? Errol had an awful, sinking feeling that they should have arrived at Uncle Hector's farm by now. Perhaps he'd missed the turnoff.

A large plop of rain slid down the back of his neck. His mom had been right about the weather, after all. He sneaked a look over at Sam, whose face was now as thunderous as the sky. Then, rounding a slight bend, he saw the comforting sight of the white farmhouse, a tendril of smoke pluming gently from its red brick chimney. Uncle Hector's house, at last!

"Well," said Errol enthusiastically, "this is it!"

"This is what?" said Sam, wiping his rain-spattered face with his sleeve.

"It. The camping spot. Our home away from home," said Errol.

"Here?" said Sam, looking around in disbelief. There was thick forest on either side of the road. The trees towered above them, suddenly making him feel very small and unsure of himself. He began to feel ridiculous in his camouflage gear and hiking boots. "It's a bit . . . wild."

"That's what makes it so special," replied Errol. "Hardly anyone has ever camped here before. We'll be like – you know – pioneers."

"We'll be wet pioneers in a minute," gulped Sam, looking at the sky. "Which way do we go now?"

"This way," said Errol brightly. He led Sam through the gate and down the track to the forest at the back of Uncle Hector's farm.

The rain was really pelting down by now. "Couldn't we just give up on this camping idea and stay in the farmhouse?" asked Sam longingly.

Errol looked shocked. "We couldn't have an adventure inside an ordinary house," he said, gasping as an icy trickle of water found its way down the inside of his collar.

"I suppose not," grumbled Sam. He tried not to think of the cheery house with its gentle tendril of smoke fading into the gray sky. "I hope your tent is waterproof."

"No problemo," said Errol, who hoped it was, too. He'd never actually been in it when it had rained. "Anyway, if the ground is wet, it will be easier to put in the tent stakes."

38

"Hmm," said Sam, inspecting the ground underfoot. It looked pretty rocky.

"Here we are," said Errol finally, as he pushed Li'l Blossom down a slight slope. "The super-special camping spot. Good, huh?"

Sam looked at the tiny strip of open space nestled among the towering trees. A dark bird flapped past his nose – at least, he hoped it was a bird. But there was something else worrying him. "Errol, what's that rushing noise?"

"What rushing noise?" asked Errol, struggling awkwardly with the buckles on his backpack.

"It's coming from over there," said Sam, pointing through the trees.

Errol put his pack down and listened. He could hear a steady whooshing sound. "Oh, that's Alligator Creek," he replied confidently.

"A-a-alligator Creek?" gulped Sam. "Are you sure?"

"Of course I'm sure," said Errol. "We've been here lots of times. My grand-father once wrestled an alligator from that creek with his bare hands. Grandma told me."

Sam hoped this was just another of Errol's stories. Still, you never could tell with Errol's family. They were all slightly eccentric. He tried not to think about the

40

alligators that might or might not be in the creek. "Let's get the tent up before everything gets soaked," he suggested.

Errol unrolled the tent and spread it out on the ground. He walked around it three times, and then once more, looking at all the ropes and poles.

"What are you doing?" asked Sam. "You do know how to put it up, don't you?"

"Of course I do," said Errol, with his fingers crossed behind his back. He grabbed the poles and began fitting them together. "Like this," he said to Sam importantly, as he began hammering the pegs into the ground. "Yes, it's just as well the ground is a bit wet. They're going in very easily." Then he wriggled inside the folds of nylon.

About twenty minutes later, the tent was up – looking a little lop-sided. The boys dragged all their gear in and sat huddled together inside, watching the rain run down the walls.

"Told you this would be fun," said Errol brightly. He poked around in the bottom of his pack. "Now, how about lunch?"

7
A Sinking Feeling

Sam felt happier with a full stomach. He worried less about what might be in the creek, and whether there were any awful creepy-crawlies waiting around outside ready to dive-bomb him.

"Now what?" he asked Errol.

"Let's play cards!" suggested Errol happily. He was really beginning to enjoy himself. "I brought some cards just in case it rained."

Sam rolled his eyes. "Okay," he said.

So Sam and Errol played cards. Then more cards. Outside the tent, the rain came down. Then it started coming down *inside* the tent. Sam was not impressed.

"Errol," he said, "I think we have a problem with our tent."

"Huh?" said Errol, concentrating on his cards. He couldn't decide whether to trade his queen or his seven.

"It's getting wet in here," said Sam firmly. He stared hard at Errol.

"Wet?" asked Errol innocently. He reached up to feel the inside of the tent.

"No Errol! Don't touch the sides!" screeched Sam.

"Wha–?" said Errol. But it was too late. More and more water seeped in through the walls. And worse – a large puddle began sliding through from the outside. Sam grabbed for his flashlight before it sank. Then he looked around for something to anchor things with, in case the whole tent started to float away!

"Oops," said Errol. He had a sinking feeling. "I guess it is getting kind of damp in here. But never mind, that's all part of the adventure. It makes camping more exciting, don't you think?"

"Hmm," said Sam, who was beginning to think that weeding and a movie would have been a much better deal.

"Let's have dinner," said Errol. "We can make a campfire, cook the hot dogs and beans, and sit around and tell each other scary stories."

"Okay," said Sam, feeling a bit more cheerful. The stories might help make up for missing out on the movie.

Errol cautiously opened the flaps of the tent and peered outside. It had almost stopped raining. "We'll need to collect some wood for the campfire," he said.

"It'll be too wet," said Sam.

"We'll rub it dry with my towel," Errol replied. "Come on, let's go. It's stopped raining now."

Sam thought of the hot dogs sizzling and spitting over a campfire. Yum. His stomach rumbled. He could smell them already. "Okay," he said. He was getting sick of playing cards, anyway.

It was getting dark. The moon shone down through the trees. In the distance, Alligator Creek whooshed steadily along. Dark birds flapped past. Something else made a strange, hooting noise.

"Did you bring the flashlight?" asked Errol. He was starting to feel just a tiny bit scared, not that he'd ever let Sam know, of course.

"The puddle got it," said Sam, peering through the gloom, "and the batteries stopped working."

"Oh," said Errol, in a small voice. "Well, soon we'll have a fire and that'll give us lots of light. I'll look for wood around here. You go that way."

Another hooting sound echoed above them through the trees. Something else made a loud chirruping sound. Then a thousand more voices joined in. Just crickets, thought Errol, starting to pick up twigs and pieces of wood.

"Eeeaaarrrrrrgggghhhhh!" shrieked something from the bushes.

Errol jumped, dropping the pieces of wood he was carrying. "Sam?" he called quietly. "Are you okay?"

"Get over here! Quick!" cried Sam.

Aliens? thought Errol, racing over to his friend. Or worse still, alligators? He began to feel slightly sick.

"Check this out!" said Sam, pointing to a gleaming skull sitting beside a long shiny skeleton. "Look, the jaws work and everything."

"Don't touch it!" yelled Errol, staring down at a long line of mean-looking ants busily climbing their way along the skeleton's vertebrae.

"Why not?" asked Sam. He was busy opening and shutting the skull's jaws, and running his thumb over the rows of sharp, pointy teeth.

"Because . . . because . . . ," Errol wasn't going to admit he was scared of it.

"What do you think it is?" asked Sam, grabbing at one of the teeth.

"It's a dinosaur," said Errol quickly.

"A what?" asked Sam.

"A dinosaur," Errol repeated, nodding his head emphatically. "That's why you *mustn't* touch it."

Sam stopped playing with the tooth, and looked in awe at the pile of bones in front of him.

"It's probably so old the bones would fall apart," said Errol.

"Really?" breathed Sam, looking at the skeleton with new respect. "A real dinosaur? Wait till I tell the kids at school. We'll be famous!"

"Let's just leave it here," said Errol, who was starting to think the skeleton looked awfully like his cat, Boris, might without any fur. He shivered.

"We'll tell Ms. Garcia about it on Monday," he said to Sam, "and we'll get her to help us contact the museum." Ms. Garcia was their science teacher. She was always telling them to be on the lookout for amazing scientific manifestations. Errol wasn't sure that this was the sort of thing she meant.

"Okay," said Sam reluctantly. "But just remember, I found it."

"Sure," said Errol generously. "Now let's get this fire going." He was thinking back to a television commercial that he'd seen once, where lots of smiling people wearing thick wool sweaters sat around a campfire. He heaped the twigs and pieces of wood together into a pyramid shape.

While Errol was busy arranging the wood, Sam sneaked back over to the bush

and grabbed the skull, then smuggled it back into the tent under his T-shirt. He was just pushing it down into his backpack when Errol called out to him, asking him for the matches.

Sam jumped guiltily, then quickly looked around. After a few moments he stuck his head through the flaps of the tent. "You know that small puddle that was here before . . ." he began.

"Yes," answered Errol, rubbing a log with his towel.

"Well, now it's become a lake, and the matches were right in the middle of it." Sam held out the soggy box.

"Oh," said Errol sadly. He put down the towel and the piece of wood. Maybe this counted as the sort of tiny problem his parents had warned him about.

It probably wasn't too late to run back up to Uncle Hector's house. They could both go inside, sit around the fire, and have a nice, warm supper in front of the television . . . Wait! What was he thinking about? Errol Flynn would *never* have given up so easily. What adventurer would give up just because he couldn't cook his supper? The mere thought of it was embarrassing.

"Well, you know, cold baked beans are actually quite tasty," he said firmly to Sam. "And in some places, my grandma said, cold hot dogs are considered a real treat, a delicacy, in fact."

Sam groaned loudly. He knew he should have chosen the movie deal. He remembered the picnic at the back of the shopping mall, and wondered why he'd *ever* let Errol talk him into this.

8
The Beast

Errol had a stomachache. It wasn't from cold beans eaten straight from the can. He'd only had a mouthful. It wasn't from cold hot dogs. There was no way he and Sam were even going to try those! They'd taken one look at the fat wobbly things and thrown them aside in disgust. No, it was from all the candy bars he and Sam had eaten to fill themselves up. He never wanted to see chocolate again in his life!

But Errol couldn't let a small pain in his stomach interfere with the really important part of the camping trip. The scary stories.

The boys were zipped snugly into their sleeping bags, which were only a little damp around all the edges. Errol was secretly glad that his mom had insisted on making him pack his fleecy pajamas. At least they were warm.

Outside the tent, the wind howled eerily through the branches. It was very, very, very dark. It was dark inside the tent, too – dark and damp. Errol curled down deeper into his sleeping bag, ready to start his first story.

He took a deep breath and began. "Once upon a time . . ."

"Get out of here!" said Sam, giving him a shove. "That's not how you start a scary story. That's how my dad talks when he's telling the baby a story."

"Oh," said Errol. "Sorry." He thought for a moment or two, then started again, his voice deep and dramatic. "They called it . . . The Beast. It was green and scaly, and everywhere it walked, it dripped slime. It had long, pointy fingers that could squeeze your throat dry – just like that!" Errol's fingers grabbed Sam's sleeping bag, right where his knees were. Sam jumped, then threw a chocolate wrapper at Errol.

"It had a round, red, slobbering mouth," Errol went on. "It lived at the bottom of a swamp. Not just any swamp, either. This swamp was the blackest, darkest, gloomiest, deepest, smelliest swamp that any hungry creature has ever crawled out of. It was . . ."

"Yeah, yeah, all right," interrupted Sam sleepily. "I get the picture about the swamp. Go on about The Beast. What sort of noises did it make?"

"Well," said Errol, who hated being interrupted when he was telling a scary story, "I was just getting to that. It made strange noises, see, really disgusting noises – sort of snuffling, slobbering noises. It snuffled and slobbered all over the place in search of food to fill its huge, green, slimy, scaly, revolting stomach. It snuffled and slobbered like a . . . Hey! Sam! Sam?"

Errol's description of the snuffling, slobbering beast was answered by a long, slow, snuffling snore. Sam, his stomach full of chocolate, had drifted off to sleep.

"Great," said Errol. He pulled the sleeping bag up to cover his ears, and turned around and around on the rocky ground, trying to make himself feel more comfortable. "Just when I was getting to the good part."

9
Time for Action

Errol woke early the next morning to find Sam gripping his arm and shaking him wildly.

"Wha-?" he muttered, peering around the tent. Every one of his bones was aching from sleeping on the cold, rocky ground.

"Shhh," whispered Sam. "Listen!"

Errol listened. He heard the wind sighing eerily through the trees. He heard the slow, steady whoosh of Alligator Creek. He heard a snuffling, slobbering noise, coming from outside the tent. A snuffling, slob . . .

"Yikes!" screamed Errol in alarm. "What was that?"

"Sssshhhh," said Sam, putting a hand over Errol's mouth. "Don't let it know we're here."

"What is it?" whispered Errol, his heart racing. He was scared, but there was no way he was going to let Sam know that.

"The thing, The Beast you were talking about last night. Listen."

Errol didn't move. He listened. The snuffling, slobbering noises were getting closer. The sides of the tent began to shake as the thing outside brushed against it. They heard a snort of rage and a loud crash as The Beast tripped over something heavy and metallic. It sounded desperate . . . for something to eat!

Errol's heart did a back flip. He was really scared now, more scared than when his cousin Edwina had stood over him dangling her pet snake by its tail, when she knew he was petrified of snakes. He was more scared than when his other cousin, Eliza, had made him stand right

at the top of the Top o' the World water
slide, when she knew that he had a
phobia about heights. He was even more
scared than when his mother had . . .

"Errol! Do something!" Sam had
wormed himself and his sleeping bag right
to the back of the tent. The snuffling,
slobbering noises were getting louder.
Worse! Some slobbering thing was trying
to get *into* the tent with them! Through
the gloom, Errol could see its red, round
mouth, nibbling at the front zipper. Pretty
soon, thought Errol, his knees clicking

like castanets, its long, scaly, revolting fingers would reach inside the tent and grab one of them. Probably him!

This was it. The end. It was all his grandma's fault. She was the one who'd insisted on them coming on this stupid camping trip in the first place.

Errol picked up a chocolate wrapper and the pencil they'd used for keeping score in the card game, and started to write a good-bye note to his parents.

Dear Mom and Dad,

Thank you for having me.

I'm sorry I wasn't able to stick around for very long as your son. Give my love to Grandma and tell her I forgive her.

Tell Scarlett she can have my collection of bottle caps if she promises to look after them as well as I did.

Signed, Errol
Your (ex) son (R.I.P.)

"Sam," he said, as he folded the note up neatly and buckled it into the map pocket of his backpack, "thanks for being my pal in times of peril and in the face of danger."

The snuffling, slobbering, round, red mouth was getting closer. Errol could see its whiskery lips. He shuddered.

"That's okay," whispered Sam, from the back of the tent. "And Errol, I'll never complain about the scariness value of your stories again."

"Thanks," said Errol. He wished he could think of some way to save them from being choked by the long, scaly, revolting fingers. He wondered what Errol Flynn would have done in a situation like this – not sat there and waited to be slimed to death, that was for sure. He looked around the tent, trying to think of a solution.

Then he saw it. A small pile of fat, wobbly, glistening things. The hot dogs! Maybe if he threw them out to The Beast slobbering away outside their tent, they might distract it for a moment.

Slowly, and very carefully, Errol unzipped the side window of the tent. Picking up the hot dogs, he heaved them out of the window, then quickly zipped it back up again.

The snuffling, slobbering noise stopped. The tent shook again as The Beast brushed against it on its way to the hot dogs. Huddled together, Sam and Errol heard a snorting, whoofling sound as The Beast greedily attacked the cold hot dogs. Errol felt his throat. He hadn't been choked. He hadn't been slimed. They were safe. For the moment.

"That was close," said Sam. "D'you think it'll come back, Err?"

Errol hoped it wouldn't. He hoped that the hot dogs – cold though they were – would be enough to satisfy The Beast's hunger. You never could tell with Beasts though.

"Aaaaarrrrrrrrrrrrgggggggghhhhhhh!" screamed Sam suddenly, as the walls of the tent shook again. "It's coming back to get us. Errol, do something else!"

Errol thought of his grandfather wrestling an alligator with his bare hands. Maybe some of that strength and courage had been passed down to him. There was only one thing to do. Face The Beast. Alone!

He could hear some strange clanking sounds coming from the direction of the campfire. The Beast must be searching for more food among the cooking equipment. Maybe if he crept up behind it while its back was turned . . .

Errol carefully unzipped the front tent flaps. The sun was really up now. It was shedding pools of light over the forest, and shining most brightly on the small pyramid of twigs and the creature that was snuffling around in the dirt.

Errol shielded his eyes for a moment against the brightness of the sun. The creature turned around and for a moment they locked eyes. "Oh," said Errol softly to himself. "So *that's* what you are."

Then, pulling himself up to his full height, Errol ran screaming toward The Beast, his arms flailing like windmills. The creature gave a snort of surprise, then stumbled off through the forest, dropping a half-chewed hot dog as it ran.

"Yaaaaaaaahhhhhhh!" yelled Errol. "And don't ever come back again!"

Sam stuck his head out of the tent, blinking in the strong light. "Did you do it?" he asked incredulously. "Did you get rid of . . . The Beast?"

"Nothing to it," said Errol modestly. Once he'd seen what was really out there, he hadn't been scared at all.

In fact, he kind of liked this sort of creature. His Uncle Hector kept four or five pigs on the farm, up near the house. This one, poor thing, must have escaped from its pen and then gotten lost in the forest. No wonder it was frantic for food.

But Errol wasn't going to tell Sam that The Beast had only been a pig, a muddy pink pig with a little curly tail, a round, red, slobbering mouth, and a whiskery chin. Not on his life!

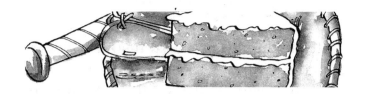

10
The Hero

The rest of the morning passed quickly. The boys packed up the camp and cleaned up the campsite – the crashing sound had been the pig tripping over Li'l Blossom, and its rear mudguard was slightly buckled. Then they went for a walk to have a look at Alligator Creek.

"So that's where your grandfather wrestled the alligator with his bare hands," breathed Sam, looking at Errol with new respect. "Brave deeds like that must run in your family."

"Yes, I suppose they must," said Errol, looking pleased. He wasn't used to people flattering him. He studied his knuckles in a modest way.

"Just wait until I tell the kids at school about this," said Sam. "Who would have thought? Errol the Peril, standing up to . . . The Beast."

He gazed admiringly at Errol for a while longer. Errol felt his face reddening, and it wasn't just from the sun.

"What did it feel like, Err? Facing the monster. Weren't you scared when you saw its green scaly claws and all that slime? Just the teensiest bit?"

"Not me," Errol replied, crossing his fingers behind his back. He wished Sam would stop talking about it.

They walked back to the clearing and got ready to leave. "I'll just drop in to see Uncle Hector on the way out," said Errol, "to tell him everything went okay." He wanted to tell his uncle about the pig escaping too, but he didn't want Sam to hear that part. "I'll only be a moment. You can wait out here, if you like."

Minutes later, he was back out on the track, holding two enormous pieces of carrot cake. (For once he was glad it wasn't chocolate.) Uncle Hector had been very pleased to learn about the missing pig, and very sorry that it had caused the boys so much trouble. Errol had told him not to worry. In fact, the pig had helped to make the whole camping trip an adventure he'd remember for the rest of his life!

Sam and Errol ate hungrily. "I told you we'd have an adventure, didn't I!" said Errol, pushing his arms into the aqua jacket just in case it rained on the way home. You never could tell.

"You bet!" said Sam. "Want me to ride Li'l Blossom for a while, Errol?"

"Er, no thanks, that's all right," said Errol. He was feeling just a tiny bit guilty about leading Sam on. "I'll race you to the bridge though."

Sam won, of course. Li'l Blossom was easy to beat, especially with a slightly buckled mudguard. After that, the boys coasted along companionably till they were close to home.

"Look!" said Sam, pointing ahead, "there's Masher McGeary."

Oh no, thought Errol. Can't he *ever* be inside?

"Just wait until I tell . . ." Sam began.

"No!" cried Errol, but it was too late. Masher had already seen them.

"Well, well, well," Masher said. He jumped down from his fence to watch Errol and Sam ride up, Li'l Blossom's back wheel squeaking sadly.

"Don't say anything about the . . ." Errol gasped, but it was too late. Sam had already pulled his bike over.

"Hey, Mash," he said, propping the bike up against the fence importantly, "bet you'll never guess what happened to us this weekend."

Masher put out a long, muscled arm and grabbed the hood of Errol's jacket as he tried to pedal past.

"Going somewhere, Peril?" he asked, sticking his foot into Li'l Blossom's front wheel, and sending Errol sprawling.

"Hey!" said Sam indignantly. "You can't do that to Errol! He's a hero. He saved me from The Beast."

Masher McGeary looked down at Errol floundering around on the path. Every time he tried to stand up, the heavy backpack made him overbalance.

"Peril? A hero?" sneered Masher. "Quit pulling my leg."

Then he noticed something white and shiny sticking out of Sam's backpack. "Hey! What's this?" he said, making a grab for it.

"Leave it alone!" cried Sam, trying to snatch it back.

Masher threw the shiny white thing high up into the air, then clumsily caught it again. "Why, Sammy Squirt?" he asked, looking at Sam's worried face. "What's so special about it?"

"It's a *dinosaur's* head," said Sam, jumping up and down, trying to reach the skull Masher was waving in front of his eyes.

"Oh sure," replied Masher, laughing nastily. "What was it, Squirt? A T-Rex? Or a velociraptor?"

"We don't know yet," answered Sam, squirming helplessly. "Errol says that we have to take it to the museum to get it identified. We're going to be famous."

"Is that so?" said Masher. "Well, sorry about that, Squirt. Finders keepers. Looks like I'm the one who's going to be famous."

He started opening the gate to go back into his yard, but something was blocking his way. Errol had finally picked himself up and was standing, shoulders squared, in front of him.

"Give it back," he said calmly, though his knees were knocking so hard that all the doors down the street were opening to see what was going on.

"Excuse me?" said Masher, getting ready to push Errol out of his way.

"I said, give it back," said Errol. "Now."

Masher stared at Errol, then burst out laughing. "Yeah? And who's going to make me? Not you, Peril." Turning back to see the reaction on Sam's face, he threw the skull high into the air.

Quick as a flash, Errol's right hand whipped out and grabbed the skull before Masher had time to catch it again. He tossed it gently over to Sam.

"Way to go!" said Sam, who'd only ever seen Errol *miss* catches on the baseball field.

"Hey!" said Masher.

"Good catch, Errol," called a new voice. It was Kate James. She and some

friends were on their way to the park at the end of Masher's street.

"Hey, Kate," cried Sam excitedly, "Do you know what Errol did this morning?"

"Hit three home runs?" asked Kate, smirking at Masher. She disliked Masher as much as Errol did.

"Nah," said Sam, "more exciting than that. He saved me from The Beast!"

"Really?" said Kate. "Looks like he's just done it again, Sam," she laughed.

Masher McGeary's face went as red as his mother's roses, and everybody saw. He stamped on the ground, and wouldn't look up again. Then, suddenly, he turned and stomped up the path to his house and slunk inside, slamming the door behind him.

Kate laughed loudly and picked up Li'l Blossom, which was lying in the gutter, its front wheel still slowly turning. "Nice bike, Errol. I might ask Mom to get me one for my birthday. We're all going up to the park to play baseball. Do you want to come?"

Errol blinked. Kate James was asking *him* to play baseball with her? After what had happened last time, she must be making some sort of joke. He was just about to excuse himself on the grounds that he had some urgent homework to do when he realized she was serious. She really *did* want him to play baseball.

And why not? he thought. Hadn't he just made the best catch of the century? Hadn't he just proved that he was fearless and brave in the face of danger? Errol dusted down his jeans and stroked the skin beneath his nose, where a mustache would be growing if he were Errol Flynn. He'd had an adventure, become a hero, and faced up to two Beasts – all in a single day.

Drawing the swashbuckling folds of his aqua jacket around his shoulders, Errol gallantly offered to let Kate ride up to the park on Li'l Blossom, while he walked proudly beside her.

Move over, Errol Flynn, thought Errol, as the little group headed off to the park. Errol Finn is here!

TITLES IN THE SERIES

SET 9A

Television Drama
Time for Sale
The Shady Deal
The Loch Ness Monster Mystery
Secrets of the Desert

SET 9B

To JJ From CC
Pandora's Box
The Birthday Disaster
The Song of the Mantis
Helping the Hoiho

SET 9C

Glumly
Rupert and the Griffin
The Tree, the Trunk, and the Tuba
Errol the Peril
Cassidy's Magic

SET 9D

Barney
Get a Grip, Pip!
Casey's Case
Dear Future
Strange Meetings

SET 10A

A Battle of Words
The Rainbow Solution
Fortune's Friend
Eureka
It's a Frog's Life

SET 10B

The Cat Burglar of Pethaven Drive
The Matchbox
In Search of the Great Bears
Many Happy Returns
Spider Relatives

SET 10C

Horrible Hank
Brian's Brilliant Career
Fernitickles
It's All in Your Mind,
    James Robert
Wing High, Gooftah

SET 10D

The Week of the Jellyhoppers
Timothy Whuffenpuffen-
    Whippersnapper
Timedetectors
Ryan's Dog Ringo
The Secret of Kiribu Tapu Lagoon